Accessorize YOURSELF!

66 PROJECTS TO PERSONALIZE YOUR LOOK

by Kara L. Laughlin,
Jennifer Phillips,
Marne Ventura, and
Debbie, Megan, and Kelly Kachidurian

Capstone Young Readers
a capstone imprint

Table of CONTENTS

YOU'RE *one of a kind,*

and your accessories should be too.

85

Super Sleepover SACK

Start with some pretty fabric, satin ribbon, and a few seams. End up with a cute drawstring bag to hold your pajamas and toiletries. Your friends won't believe you made it!

MATERIALS:

Tip: The selvedge edge of fabric is finished by the manufacturer so it won't ravel. Selvedges should be trimmed away before you begin a project because they are thicker than the rest of the fabric.

1. Trim off two inches of the selvedge side of the fabric.
2. Hem one long raw edge of the fabric by folding it in ½-inch (1.3-cm), ironing, and sewing in place.
3. Fold the fabric in half vertically. Sew a ½-inch seam across the bottom and up the side. Stop 4 inches (10.2 cm) before the top edge. Backstitch.
4. Fold the top edge down 2 inches (2.5 cm). Pin. Sew close to the top edge and along the lower edge to form a casing.

Friendship STACKS

For a spin on the classic friendship bracelet, consider a friendship anklet instead. Design your anklets to either match or complement each other. You can even make them in a few different colors to go with everything in your wardrobe.

MATERIALS:

Tip: Save this project for your next sleepover. Then you and your friends can make them together.

1. Cut three pieces of cording 20 inches (50.8 cm) long.
2. Fold the cording in half and thread the folded portion through the metal ring. Feed the cording through to loop to secure it on the ring.
3. Braid one side of the cord until you reach the end of the bracelet.
4. Trim the ends of the cords to make them even. Glue the ends and push them into the end caps. Let dry.
5. Repeat steps 3–4 to add three more to added cords. You should have two cords on each side of the metal ring.
6. Use jump rings to attach clamps to the end caps.

127

DESIGN WEARABLE WORKS OF ART IN JUST MINUTES!

Create jewelry, scarves, bags, hats, and more! You'll have everything you need to make must-have masterpieces.

Be inspired to add your own twists to the projects in this book. Make each accessory uniquely yours!

66 PROJECTS

97

45

Accessorize
YOURSELF!

66 PROJECTS TO PERSONALIZE YOUR LOOK

From Drink TO 'DO

Did you know that most disposable drinking cups are made from shrinkable plastic? It's true! So the next time you're at a picnic or pool party, bring home your cup. No one will ever believe your latest accessory started as a drink holder!

MATERIALS:

parchment paper
baking sheet
red #6 plastic cup
permanent markers
hole punch

scissors
empty 16-ounce
   (0.5-liter) jar
bamboo skewer

Tip: Use small, 1-ounce (29.6-milliliter) cups to make a barrette version of this project.

1. Preheat oven to 250 degrees Fahrenheit (120 degrees Celsius). Lay a piece of parchment paper on a baking sheet.

2. Draw a fun design on the sides of your cup with permanent markers.

3. Punch two holes on opposite sides of the cup about ½ inch (1.3 centimeters) from the rim.

4. Carefully cut away the bottom of the cup.

5. Set the cup bottom up on the parchment paper and put it in the oven.

6. The cup will collapse into a puffy disk in 3 to 5 minutes. As soon as it does, remove it from the oven. Use a potholder to curve it around the sides of your jar.

7. Trim your bamboo skewer to 6 inches (15.2 cm).

8. Once the cup has cooled, slide the skewer though the holes. (You may need to re-punch the holes.)

MATERIALS:

scissors
stiffened craft felt
hair comb
vintage buttons
   and jewelry

felt glue
needle and clear nylon
   thread or fishing line

Vintage GLAMOUR

A few pieces of old costume jewelry or vintage buttons can transform hair combs from blah to bling. Search thrift stores and yard sales for your finds. Limit choices to one or two main colors to keep the project glam, not gaudy.

> *Tip: If combs don't work well in your hair, decorate a headband instead. Sew a loop of elastic to the back of the felt and slide it onto a plastic headband. You can keep it removable or glue it in place.*

1. Cut a piece of stiffened felt the same length as your hair comb.

2. Arrange buttons and jewelry pieces in a pattern on the felt. Use felt glue to glue into place. Let dry.

3. Cut away the extra felt from around the buttons and jewelry pieces.

4. Thread needle with thread or fishing line and secure the knot with felt glue.

5. Sew the felt to the comb by wrapping the thread around the top of the comb. Sew all the way across the comb and back to be sure the felt is secure. Knot the thread and cut off any excess.

6. Lay down a line of felt glue where the felt meets the top of the comb. Let the glue dry before wearing.

Boho Bling HAIRBAND

Turban-style hair wraps are super comfy and look great.
This one adds to the swag factor with a sparkly chain
and fabric you dye yourself.

MATERIALS:

tape measure
wire cutter
metal chain
beaded chain
scissors

knit cotton fabric
craft glue
no-boil fabric dye
needle and thread

Tip: Don't use the stovetop
method to dye the fabric.
It could melt the glue.

1. Measure the widest part of your head. Use the wire cutter to cut the metal and beaded chains to this measurement. Then cut a piece of cotton fabric, using the measurement for the length and 5 inches (12.7 cm) for the width.

2. Spread the fabric out on a work surface and squeeze glue in a fun pattern onto the cloth. Let the glue dry overnight.

3. Dye your cloth according to the package instructions. If some fabric puffs up while you're dying, use a wooden spoon or butter knife to push the air pocket to the edge of the fabric. That should release the bubble and let the fabric sink back into the dye. When your fabric is dyed and rinsed, but still damp, peel off the glue.

4. Wash the fabric and let it dry completely before sewing.

5. Fold your fabric along its length so that the right side of the pattern is on the inside. Sew the edges together lengthwise to make a tube. Turn the tube right-side-out.

6. Lay the chains on the fabric in an X. Sew them to the fabric where the chains cross. Sew the ends of the chains to the ends of the fabric ½ inch from the raw edges of the fabric.

7. Tuck ½ inch (1.3 cm) of one side of the tube into the other. Fold the outside fabric about ¼ inch (0.6 cm) under and sew the fabric together to make a circle.

Punchy Puff HEADBAND

Who knew paper could be this pretty—and strong?
This is a great everyday headband for when you
want to just add a little punch to your 'do.

3

MATERIALS:

large cooking pot
serrated knife or craft saw
5-inch (12.7-cm) wooden
   embroidery hoop
bowl or jar, about 4 inches
   (10.2 cm) wide
flower-shaped paper punch

scrapbooking paper in several
   contrasting colors
1 inch (2.5 cm) round
   paper punch
½-inch (1.3-cm) round
   paper punch
dimensional decoupage glue

1. Fill the pot about halfway with water. Then bring the water to a boil.

2. Cut the metal parts off of the outer ring of the embroidery hoop. Boil the hoop in the water until it's flexible, about 20 minutes.

3. Use tongs to remove hoop from the water and rinse it in cold water until it's cool enough to handle. Bend the hoop and place the ends in the bowl or jar. Leave the hoop in the jar until it's completely dry. This could take several hours, or even overnight.

4. Punch 6 flowers from each sheet of scrapbooking paper. Set the flowers on a protected work surface. Cover the flowers with dimensional decoupage.

5. Repeat step 4 with the round paper punches. Cover the circles with dimensional decoupage. Let the flowers and the circles dry completely.

6. Use decoupage glue to attach the larger circles to the flowers, and the flowers and smaller circles to the headband. Use additional glue along the underside of the flowers for added stability. Let dry completely.

MATERIALS:

metal blanks with
 beading holes
pencil
stamping block or flat
 piece of metal

alphabet metal stamping kit
hammer
jump ring
small bead
metal choker necklace

Make Your MARK

Metal stamping is easier than you think! A set of stamps, a few swings of your hammer, and you've got a personalized pendant. When you see how easy they are, you'll be making them for all of your friends.

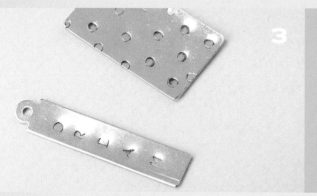

3

Tips: Practice makes perfect! Experiment with a throwaway blank before diving in.

Stamping kits and blanks can be found at craft stores. Check sales and use store coupons to get the best deals.

1. Lightly mark the metal blank with a pencil to make sure your letters will be centered and evenly spaced. If your blanks are small, a piece or two of clear tape along the edges can help keep the blanks in place.

2. Stamp your design onto the blank. Hold the stamp straight over the blank. Hold the hammer near the head, and gently hammer the stamp once.

3. Continue stamping until the blank is decorated to your liking. Use a damp rag to rub off the pencil marks from step 1.

4. Thread the bead onto the jump ring. Then thread the metal blank onto the jump ring.

5. Hang your stamped charm off the metal choker necklace.

MATERIALS:

1-inch (2.5-cm) circle
    paper punch
playing cards
scissors
embossing fluid
metallic embossing powder
paintbrush

hair dryer
pushpin
clear nail polish
jewelry pliers
jump rings
12-inch (30.5-cm) piece
    of necklace chain

Dealing Up DESIGN

The next time you discover a few cards missing from your favorite deck, don't toss the rest. Show off the detailed designs by incorporating them into this scalloped necklace.

1. Punch 8 circles from playing cards. Then cut them in half.

2. Pour embossing fluid onto a paper plate. Dip the cut edges of the half circles into the fluid. Then dip the edges in embossing powder. Use a dry paintbrush to dust off any excess powder. Heat the powder with a hair dryer until the powder melts and turns shiny.

3. Use a pushpin to poke a hole in each of the top corners of the card pieces. Add a drop of clear nail polish to each hole. Let dry.

4. Use jewelry pliers to thread a jump ring through one of the holes. Use the jump rings to join 10 card pieces.

5. Repeat to make a second chain of six card pieces. Attach the ends of the chains to one another.

6. Attach the necklace chain to the jump rings at the ends of the card pieces.

Tip: Open and close those jump rings right! Use two pairs of pliers and twist the ends perpendicular to the ring. When you twist back to close, wobbling the ends will help keep it closed.

MATERIALS:

craft glue
pendant with bezel setting
foil-lined seed beads, size 12
tweezers
loose seed beads

sponge
powdered tile grout or
  mosaic grout
decorative chain or string
  of seed beads with a clasp

Magical MOSAIC

Don't you just love it when all the little things come together? Foil-lined beads make this pendant sparkle, and mosaic grout keeps them in place.

Tip: If you don't have grout handy, you can use clear resin. Be sure to pop any air bubbles before you let the resin dry.

1. Use glue to draw a shape on the inside of the bezel setting.

2. Lay your beads on the glue. Use tweezers to nudge the string into a smooth shape. Leave them strung and let the glue dry.

3. Remove the excess beads from your design. Fill the rest of the bezel setting with glue, and add loose beads in a second color to cover the rest of the bezel setting. Let dry.

4. Follow package instructions to mix grout. Apply grout evenly to the beads. It's okay if the beads don't show through or look dusty.

5. Allow the grout to dry for one hour. Wipe off excess grout with a damp sponge.

6. Let grout set for another day, then wipe again with a damp sponge.

7. Hang the pendant on a chain or string of beads.

Tip: If you don't have grout handy, you can use clear resin. Be sure to pop any air bubbles before you let the resin dry.

MATERIALS:

round size 8 seed beads
   (about 90)
embroidery thread

small tapestry needle
narrow crochet hook
   (size E/4 or smaller)

Beauty and the BEADS

Wear this fiber necklace long, or wrap it around your neck a few times for a layered look. It's amazing how pretty slipping one loop over another can be—when you do it several hundred times!

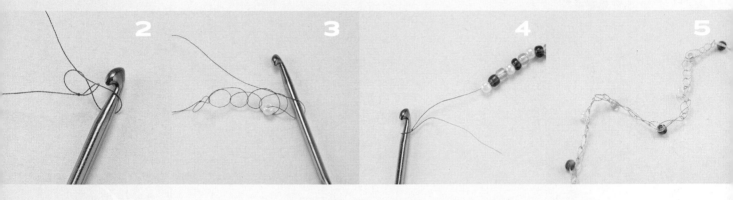

1. Thread beads onto your spool of embroidery thread with your beading needle.

2. Tie a loop in the end of the thread, and put the loop on your crochet hook.

3. Twist thread around your crochet hook and slip the first loop off of the hook. This is a single crochet.

4. After five single crochets, push a bead up so that it gets wrapped around the hook. When you slip the loop off the hook, slip the loop over the bead as well.

5. Continue making single crochets, and adding a bead every fifth stitch, until the necklace measures 48 inches (122 cm).

6. Slip the hook back into the beginning of your chain. Wrap the hook as usual, and then slip both loops off of hook. Cut the thread away from the spool and pull the end through.

7. With your tapestry needle, weave the end of the thread back into the necklace.

Tip: Get a very unique look with different materials. Try using satin or organza ribbon with ¼ inch (0.6 cm) painted glass beads for a more romantic look. You can even crochet a chain from beading wire.

small lock charm
48 inch (122 cm) chain with
   round links at least ⅜ inch
   (1 cm) in diameter

¼-inch- (0.6-cm-) wide
   leather cord
coordinating key charm
two ¼-inch (0.6-cm) beads

Lariat Lock DOWN

This lariat necklace is key to having a little versatility in your jewelry wardrobe. Since it adjusts to any neckline, you'll always have a lock on a great look.

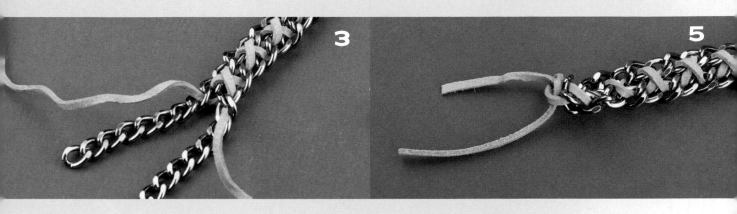

1. Slip the lock charm onto the chain and fold the chain so that the ends are together with the lock hanging at the other end.

2. Cut a 96-inch (2.4-meter) piece of cord. Starting at the lock end, thread the cord through links on either side of the chain. Even out the cord so that both ends are the same length.

3. Thread the left cord down through the next open link on the right chain. Then thread the right cord down the next open link on the left chain.

4. Your cord should be on the underside of the chain. Cross the cords and send them back up through the next links.

5. Continue lacing the cord through the chain all the way down. Tie a knot, but do not cut the ends.

6. Slip the working end of the chain through the lock's handle. Then tie the key to the working end of the chain.

7. Tie a bead to the end of each cord, then cut off the end.

MATERIALS:

polymer clay
drinking straws cut into
  3-inch (7.6-cm) pieces
aluminum foil
baking sheet
scissors
20-inch- (50.8-cm-) long chain

20-inch-long piece of
  ½-inch- (1.3-cm-) wide ribbon
4 ribbon crimps
14-mm jump rings
necklace clasp
pendant

In a TWIST

Here's a new twist on a romantic ribbon necklace. The handmade spiral beads add a splash of color and fun—perfect for a night out with friends.

1. Pull off a marble-sized piece of polymer clay, and knead it until it's soft.

2. Roll the clay into a snake about ¼ inch (0.6 cm) in diameter. Wrap the snake in a tight spiral around a drinking straw, and set onto a foil-lined baking sheet.

3. Repeat steps 1 and 2 to make three more beads.

4. Bake the clay beads according to the package instructions.

5. When the beads have baked and cooled, slide them off of the straws.

6. Gather the two ribbons and chain together. Insert them into the top of a spiral bead. Twist the spiral around the ribbon and chain until they are completely inside the spiral. Add the rest of your beads the same way.

7. Add a ribbon crimp to each of your ribbon ends.

8. Attach the ribbon crimps and chain to your clasp with a jump ring. Use another jump ring to attach the pendant.

Tip: These beads work well alone too! Before you cure them, make loops in the ends for jump rings. You can cluster five or seven together for a squiggly pendant, or link them together lengthwise for a fun bracelet.

MATERIALS:

polymer clay	baking sheet
penknife	jewelry glue
aluminum foil	earring posts

Really ROSY

These delicate rose earrings look intricate, but they are surprisingly simple to make. Use them to add a bit of understated style to a T-shirt and jeans. Pair them with an updo and a strappy dress for a special night out.

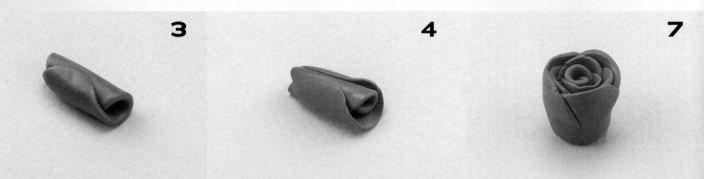

3   **4**   **7**

1. Knead a marble-sized piece of polymer clay until soft.

2. Break the clay into 16 equal balls.

3. Press one ball into a flat disk. Gently roll this disk up to make the central spiral of your rose.

4. Flatten another ball and curl it around the spiral.

5. Add six more petals to your rose. Always add in the same direction, and overlap the petals.

6. Repeat steps 3–5 to make a second rose.

7. Carefully cut the bottom of each rose to make it sit flat.

8. Set the roses onto a foil-lined baking sheet. Cure your roses in the oven according to package instructions.

9. When your roses have cooled completely, glue them to earring posts.

Tip: Now that you can make clay roses, add a matching bracelet! Make 8 to 12 roses, but before you bake them, press closed jump rings into opposite sides of each rose. Connect the roses with more jump rings and add a clasp.

MATERIALS:

16 to 20 thin gauge (8- to 12-mm) jump rings

two 1-inch- (2.5-cm-) long pieces of brass chain, ⅛ inch (0.3 cm) in diameter

two 1 ½-inch- (3.8-cm-) long pieces of brass chain, ⅛ inch (0.3 cm) in diameter

two 2 ½-inch- (6.4-cm-) long pieces of silver chain, ¼ inch (0.6-cm) in diameter

four 1 ¼-inch- (3.2-cm-) long peices of silver chain, ⅛ (0.3 cm) inch in diameter

two 1 ¼-inch- (3.2-cm-) long pieces of copper chain, ¼ inch (0.6 cm) in diameter

two 2-inch- (5-cm-) long pieces of copper chain, ¼ (0.6 cm) inch in diameter

two 2-inch- (5-cm-) long pieces of copper chain, ⅛ inch (0.3 cm) in diameter

two 1 ½ inch- (3.8-cm-) long pieces of copper chain, ⅛ inch (0.3 cm) in diameter

2 earring frames

two pairs jewelry pliers

6 top-drilled crystal teardrop beads

ear wires

Crystal CHANDELIERS

When your outfit calls for high drama, break out these chandelier earrings. The mixed metals mean you can wear them with most fashion styles. Bonus: They're a great way to upcycle old necklaces.

1. Use a jump ring to attach a 1-inch- (2.5-cm-) long piece of brass chain to a 1.25-inch (3.2-cm) piece of silver chain.

2. Repeat to attach a 1.25-inch- (3.2-cm-) long piece of silver chain with a matching piece of copper chain. Make pairs of 1.5-inch (3.8-cm) chain and 2-inch (5.1-cm) chain in the same way.

3. Arrange your chain pairs so that the shorter pieces are on the outside and the longer ones are in the center. You will have one 2.5-inch (6.4-cm) piece of silver chain in the center.

4. Use the jump ring to attach the chains to the earring frame through the holes on the bottom.

5. Thread a jump ring through one of the crystal beads. Attach the bead to the bottom of the longest chain. Attach two more crystal beads to the next longest chains.

6. Hang your earring on the loop at the bottom of the ear wire. Use pliers to close up the loop.

7. Repeat steps 1–6 to make a second earring.

Tip: For a retro look, skip the crystals and paint the chains with brightly colored nail polish or enamel paint.

MATERIALS:

20-gauge jewelry wire
wooden spool, about 1 inch
    (2.5 cm) in diameter
round-nosed jewelry pliers
flat-nosed or nylon-tipped pliers

2 eye pins
2 large beads
16 seed beads
nail file
hammer

Ten-Minute HOOPS

Hoops are the blue jeans of jewelry—you can wear them every day, and they go with anything. Make a few pairs with different beads, and you'll always have something to wear with your favorite outfits.

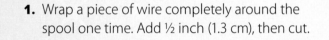

4

1. Wrap a piece of wire completely around the spool one time. Add ½ inch (1.3 cm), then cut.

2. With a round-nosed pliers, turn the extra half inch of wire into a loop.

3. Grasp the loop with a flat-nosed pliers and bend it away from the hoop at a 45-degree angle. Set aside.

4. Thread a eye pin through one of the large beads. Use round-nosed pliers to make a loop at the top of the eye pin.

5. String four seed beads onto the hoop. Add the large bead. Then string four more seed beads.

6. Use the flat-nosed pliers to bend up the free end of the hoop. Trim off any extra wire and smooth the cut end with a nail file.

7. Gently hammer each side of the hoop flat.

8. Repeat steps 1–7 for the second earring.

TEMPER, TEMPER!

Wire has to be bendy enough to work with, but not so bendy that it loses its shape. Fortunately, there's a way to have your wire flexible when you're working it, and firm when you finish. It's called tempering.

Here are a few ways to temper your jewelry wire:

• pull the wire straight with nylon-nosed pliers

• bend it as you work with it

• hammer it

Be careful! If you work the metal too much, it becomes brittle and can break.

MATERIALS:

wool roving in two colors
hot water
dish soap
needle that will fit through the
    holes in your beads

thread
seed beads
closed jump rings
ear wires

Felting FUN

When you think of wool, you probably think sweaters or socks. But wool is great for jewelry too. It's strong, inexpensive, and easy to decorate. These earrings start off as little more than fluff. With a little work, though, you'll have bits of felt perfect for fashion.

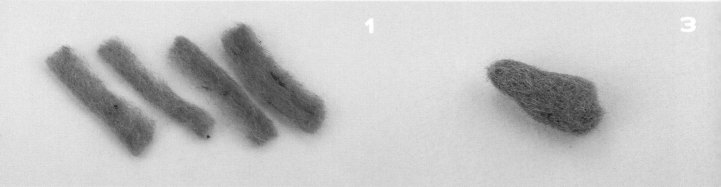

1. Pull four to five pieces of wool roving into a strip about 3 inches (7.6 cm) by ½ inch (1.3 cm). Tie the wool into a loose knot.

2. Dip the wool in hot, soapy water. Roll the knot around in your hands for about 15 minutes, until it's tight and round.

3. Pull about twice as much roving as before and dip it in the water. Make a long teardrop shape by gently rolling the wool back and forth.

4. Repeat steps 1–3 for the second earring. Allow felted pieces to dry for two days.

5. Sew seed beads onto the felt pieces.

6. Attach closed jump rings to the top and bottom of each felt ball.

7. Sew each teardrop to the bottom jump rings. Attach earring wires to the top jump rings.

Tip: If your wool shapes keep breaking open, start over with a new piece of roving and be gentler when you roll it. Too much pressure will felt the piece before it has time to knit together into the shape that you want.

MATERIALS:

nail polish in two
   contrasting colors
4 lock washers, ½ inch
   (1.3 cm) in diameter

beads
silk or nylon beading
   cord and needle
ear wires

Sunburst DANGLES

Jewelry supplies don't just come from the craft store. These earrings are made of lock washers, found at hardware and home improvement stores. Make these baubles bright with a pop of color and a few pretty beads.

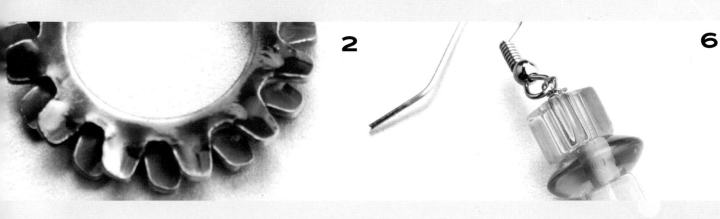

2

6

1. Use nail polish to paint one pair of washers. Paint the other pair of washers with the second color. Let dry.

2. Position one lock washer over another of the other color. Their prongs should alternate to make a two-color starburst shape.

3. Fold an 18-inch (45.7-cm) piece of beading cord in half. Slip the center through one pair of lock washers, and then pass the ends through to make a slipknot.

4. Tie one end of the cord to the needle. Thread three beads onto the cord, then pass the needle through an ear wire. Send the needle back down through the beads and tie it to the other end of the beading cord.

5. Send the needle back up through the beads, and cut the cord between two beads so that the end disappears between them.

6. Thread the other end of the beading cord and hide its end between the beads in the same way.

7. Repeat steps 2–6 for the second earring, alternating which color washer is on top, if desired.

SOURCING OUTSIDE THE BOX

Hardware stores aren't the only places hiding jewelry equipment in plain sight! Next time you're in one of these stores, keep a lookout for these great components:

hardware store: washers, nuts, zip ties, fan pulls, tile spacers, tile grout, bungee cords, keys, chains

office supply store: metal brads, paper clips, metal and paper price tags, pencils, safety pins

fabric store: zippers, buttons, buckles, plastic cord guide rings, ribbons, fringe, tassels

electronics store: resistors, LED lights, copper wire, electrical tape, PVC tape

Quirky Cork POSTS

Slices of cork are the perfect canvases for rubber stamps and ink. These earrings are so adaptable, you could make several pairs with completely different looks.

MATERIALS:

cork bottle stopper
serrated knife
alcohol ink
patterned rubber stamp
    and stamp pad
permanent markers
tissue paper
decoupage glue

two ¼-inch (0.6-cm)
    eye screws or head pins
jewelry glue
2 round or oval beads
2 eye pins
round-nosed pliers
earring posts and backs

4

1. Cut two ⅛-inch- (0.3-cm-) thick pieces of cork with a serrated knife.

2. Add a drop of alcohol ink to two or three places on the cork disks. Let dry.

3. Ink your rubber stamp and press it onto the cork so that the top half of the cork is covered in the pattern. Use permanent markers to color in the pattern on the cork, if desired.

4. Tear two pieces of tissue paper into 1 inch (2.5 cm) squares. Lay the tissue paper across the bottom halves of the corks. Paint the paper with decoupage glue and wrap the edges around the cork. Let dry.

5. Gently twist eye screws into the bottom edges of the cork disks. Secure with a dot of jewelry glue.

6. Thread beads onto the eye pins. Use round-nosed pliers to loop them through the eye screw.

7. Secure earring posts to the backs of the cork circles with jewelry glue.

MATERIALS:

alcohol inks in two colors
2 metal blanks with a hole
    at the top
cotton swabs
jump rings
ear wires

chandelier findings with
    three links
14 ⅛-inch (0.3-cm) beads
14 head pins
round-nosed pliers

Rainy Day DANGLES

*Need a lift on a gray day? Try on some fab earrings!
The back disks of these earrings may look like puddles in
the rain, but with these pretty dangles in your ears, you'll
be walking on sunshine all day long.*

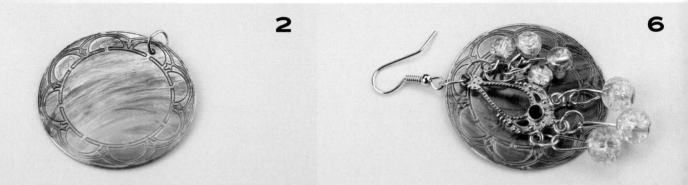

2

6

1. Place one drop of alcohol ink onto each blank. Add one or two drops of the other color. Use a cotton swab to push the ink around on the metal. When you have the look you want, let it dry.

2. Attach a jump ring to the top of a blank.

3. Thread an earring wire and a chandelier finding onto the jump ring. Thread another jump ring onto the chandelier finding.

4. Place a bead on a head pin, then use the pliers to close the head pin. Repeat to make six more beads.

5. Hang one bead off the jump ring from step 2. Add three more beads to the second jump ring.

6. Use more jump rings to hang a bead onto each of the chandelier finding's links.

Headband HAT

A single headband makes a great accessory. Stack several together to make a slouchy hat that's beyond amazing.

2

MATERIALS:

five fabric headbands
straight pins
needle and thread
felt flowers

1. Decide the order for stacking the headbands. Put the widest one on the bottom.

2. Pin the bottom two headbands together, overlapping by ¼ inch (0.6 cm). Whip stitch the pinned edges together. If one band is a little wider than the other, ease the extra fabric into gentle folds as you stitch.

3. Continue pinning and stitching until all the headbands are attached.

4. Make a loose stitch around the top of the hat. Carefully pull the thread tight to cinch the edges and sew them closed.

5. Sew on the felt flowers.

Tip: For an even slouchier hat, add more headbands.

MATERIALS:

jewelry chain with medium
  or large links
scissors
bowler or top hat
thin ribbon
sewing needle with large eye

thin silver jewelry wire
needle-nosed pliers
feathers
small metal gears and other
  watch parts
clear fabric glue

Steampunk STYLE

Steampunk fashion is a modern nod to Victorian-era science fiction and the introduction of steam-powered machines. The look mixes historical and futuristic fashion for a creative and stylish combination.

Tip: Rather have the real thing? Find replicas of cameo pendants, charms, and gadgets at craft stores or thrift stores. Look for watch parts, gears, washers, or anything else that represents steampunk style.

1. Cut jewelry chain to wrap twice around the hat base. Cut ribbon to same length, plus 10 inches (25 cm).

2. Fold chain in half. Knot the ribbon through the links at one end, leaving 2 inches (5 cm) hanging out. Connect the two chain rows by threading ribbon up and down through the links using the sewing needle (if using a thick ribbon, skip some links as you go). Knot the ribbon ends together and slide onto the hat base.

3. Cut two lengths of wire 3 to 6 inches (7.6 to 15.2 cm). Use the pliers to twist one end of the wire into a small hook. Continue twisting the wire until you have a spiral.

4. Decide how you want the feathers, gears, and watch parts placed. When you're happy with the design, glue them onto the hat. Use the metal pieces to hold the twisted wire from step 3 in place.

MATERIALS:

scissors
colorful fabric with large design
straw hat
decoupage glue
foam brush
waterproof fabric sealant
leather cord or ribbon

Wear it WESTERN

Are you convinced a cowgirl hat only looks good on the ranch? Think again! With colorful fabric and a little bit of leather, you'll have a fun weekend hat that works anywhere.

5

Tip: If you have a hard time cutting out the designs or your fabric frays a lot, brush the fabric with decoupage and let dry. The decoupage will make the fabric more stiff and easier to cut.

1. Cut the designs out of the fabric.

2. Brush a thin layer of decoupage glue onto the hat and position a fabric design on top. Brush a thin layer of decoupage glue on top of the fabric. Repeat until all of the fabric is attached. Let dry.

3. Place the hat in a well-ventilated area and on a protected work surface. Spray with waterproof sealant. Let dry.

4. Measure the hat's circumference. Cut three pieces of leather cord or ribbon the length of the circumference plus 6 inches (15.2 cm).

5. Secure leather or ribbon ends on one side with a knot and make a braid. Fit the braid around the hat base. Overlap the ends and secure with a knot, trimming off any excess.

Patchwork WONDER

Bring out your playful side. Bold strips of canvas and trim add instant fun to a fedora. The more mismatched the look, the better.

MATERIALS:

canvas fabrics in several colors and patterns
scissors
fedora hat
foam brush
fabric glue
decorative ribbon
waterproof fabric sealant
accent piece, such as a button, feather, brooch, pin, or flower

Tip: If you don't have a spare fedora, fear not. You can use the same technique on a baseball cap or old straw hat.

1. Cut out fabric strips in varying widths. The strips should all be about 4 inches (10.2 cm) long. You should have enough pieces to cover the top of the hat. A typical hat will need about 20 strips.

2. Brush fabric glue onto the hat. Attach strips of fabric to the sides of the hat, and the hat's brim. Fold excess fabric under the brim and glue in place. Work in small sections to keep the glue from getting too dried out.

3. Continue adding fabric strips until the entire hat is covered.

4. Glue ribbon around the hat's brim.

5. In a well-ventilated area, spray with sealant and let dry.

6. Add the accent piece by sewing, pinning, or gluing it into place as needed.

MATERIALS:

measuring tape
scissors
fabric

sewing machine or needle
    and thread
flower embellishment

Band TOGETHER

Take a twist on the traditional turban-style headband with this simple and easy-to-stitch project. Let people get a good look at your pretty profile.

4

Tip: Use any stretchy fabric for this craft, such as fleece, cotton, or lycra. You can also use old T-shirts, swimsuits, or blankets.

1. Measure and cut a piece of fabric 6 by 22 inches (15.2 by 55.9 cm).

2. Fold the fabric vertically, with the right sides together. Sew the long sides of the fabric together.

3. Repeat steps 1 and 2 to make a second fabric tube.

4. Turn the fabric tubes right-side-out. Fold them in half, and then loop them around each other.

5. Sew the edges of the tubes together. Add embellishment, if desired.

MATERIALS:

felt
two men's ties
chalk
scissors
pins
needle and thread or sewing machine

Obi BELT

Obi is the Japanese word for sash. Put a modern twist on the obi traditionally worn with kimonos. It's a great way to glam up an older outfit.

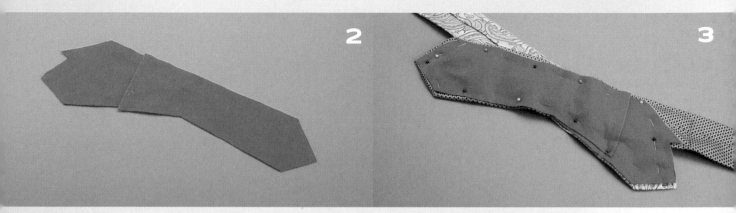

1. Set the felt on your work surface. Lay the ties flat on top of the felt. Overlap the wide ends of the ties, and pin together.

2. Trace the ties' shape from the tips to the edge where they overlap onto the felt. Then cut out the felt.

3. Pin the felt to the back of the ties. Then sew the felt and the ties together. Be sure to sew around the entire felt piece. Remove pins as you sew.

4. To wear, start with the wide end of the ties in the front. Loop the thin ends around your body, and bring them back around to tie a knot in the front.

Tip: Thrift stores are great places to find fun ties at bargain prices.

Comic Craze BELT

Turn a belt into a statement about your favorite graphic novel, manga, or anime heroes. Cut out some comics and get ready to create this perfectly paneled conversation starter.

MATERIALS:

old comic books
leather or vinyl belt
decoupage glue
foam brush
seam ripper

Tip: To add more comic book wearables to your closet, use this technique on other accessories like shoes and bracelets. Spray shoes with acrylic sealant before wearing.

1. Find and cut out enough images to cover the entire belt.

2. Brush a layer of decoupage glue onto the belt in small sections. Attach paper strips. Let dry.

3. Brush a thin layer of decoupage glue on top of the belt. Let dry.

4. Continue adding layers of decoupage until the belt is as smooth as possible. Let layers dry before adding the next.

5. Use the seam ripper to poke and uncover belt holes.

MATERIALS:

old pair of jeans
scissors
seam ripper
straight pins
sewing machine or
   needle and thread

sticky-back hook and
   loop closures
appliqués, metallic
   buttons, studs, or beads
grommets
decorative lace ribbon

Fashion Meets
FUNCTION BELT

Need a place to store your stuff? With this cute denim belt complete with hidden pockets, you can leave your purse behind.

1. Cut off both pant legs and remove seams. Use a seam ripper to remove and keep any cool pockets or decorative details.

2. Measure and cut out a length of jean material that fits around your waist plus 2 inches (5 cm). The width should be about 10 inches (25.4 cm). You can sew together sections to make a long enough piece if needed. Since jean legs curve in toward the top, you may need to lay the pieces flat and even them out.

3. Fold the material in half lengthwise with the right sides facing in. Whip stitch the short sides.

4. Fold down the edges all around the top of the belt to create an inside hem and whip stitch in place. Turn the piece inside out so the right sides show. Sew straight up the short sides of the belt to create pocket dividers.

5. Apply sticky-back hook and loop closures at the top of the pockets. Add appliqués, decorative buttons, studs, or beads.

6. Determine how fitted you want the belt and mark a spot on one end for a fastener hole. Use a seam ripper to create a small hole.

7. Follow package instructions to attach the grommet. Use decorative lace ribbon to tie the belt shut.

Chunky CLASS

Mix book rings and chunky beads for a fun, flexible belt. Pair it with jeans or a cute summer dress.

MATERIALS:

nail polish in several colors
1-inch (2.5-cm) book rings (enough to fit
    around your waist plus an extra inch)
short, chunky beads with wide openings
2-inch (5-cm) book ring, or a metal
    shower ring
large lobster clasp

Tip: You need beads that will easily slide onto the rings. Look for beads with holes at least ¼ inch (0.6 cm) wide and less than ½ inch (1.3 cm) long. Longer beads will get stuck on the curved rings.

1. Use nail polish to paint the book rings in a variety of colors. Let dry.

2. Add four beads to a 1-inch ring and snap it closed.

3. String beads onto a second ring. Then attach the two rings. Repeat until the belt is the length you want.

4. When you reach the end of your belt, close it with the 2-inch ring. Add beads to the ring but leave 1 inch without beads so there's space to attach and fasten and unfasten the lobster clasp.

MATERIALS:

measuring tape
belt buckle
scissors
fabric
pins

sewing machine or
   needle and thread
iron
seam ripper

Tailored for ONE

Can't find just the right belt in the store? No worries.
Make your own to match your mood and style.

1. Measure your waist plus 10 inches (25.4 cm) for the belt length. Measure the width of the bar in the middle of the belt buckle. Multiply this number by two and add another inch. This will be the belt's width. Cut out a fabric strip in the dimensions you need.

2. Fold belt in half lengthwise with right sides together. Pin and sew long edge and one short end with a ½-inch (1.3-cm) seam. If you are hand sewing, use a back stitch for extra strength.

3. Turn belt right-side-out. Use an iron to flatten the belt.

4. Use the seam ripper to cut a small centered hole 1.5 inches (3.8 cm) below the edge of the open short end. Sew a tight buttonhole stitch around the hole to keep the edges from fraying.

5. Put a horizontal basting stitch ¼-inch (0.6-cm) below this same open edge.

6. Slip the end with the basting stitch through the buckle. Insert the buckle prong through the belt hole. The prong should lay flat pointing out from the end of the belt.

7. Turn the belt over and fold under the end fabric at the basting stitch. Whip stitch the fold in place. Remove the basting stitch.

8. Try on the belt and mark where you want more belt holes to go. Repeat the steps to add more buttonhole-stitched openings.

Tip: Belt buckle feel too bare? Wrap it with yarn! Tie one end of the yarn to the buckle. Then wrap the yarn, tying where necessary. When done, trim off the extra pieces around any knots, push the knots to the underside and use a little craft glue to secure any ends.

Modern ART

Want a way to show off your artistic side?
Sometimes the best art isn't hung on the wall.

MATERIALS:

pinking shears
medium-weight jersey
  knit fabric
measuring tape
straight pins
stencils
fabric paint and brushes

fabric glue
tweezers
sequins
small seed beads
felt or fabric flowers
needle and thread
ribbon or lace

Tip: Don't have pinking shears? You can either leave the scarf edges unfinished or sew a narrow hem.

1. Use pinking shears to cut fabric to 12 inches by 60 inches (30.5 by 152.4 cm).

2. Measure 14 inches (35.6 cm) from the short edges and mark with straight pins.

3. Place a stencil on the fabric and brush on paint. Use different stencils and paints to add a variety of images on both bottom sections of the scarf. Let dry.

4. Squeeze a thin layer of glue onto one of the shapes. Use tweezers to attach sequins or beads. Add flowers; attach with a few stitches for extra stability. Let glue dry.

5. Glue the ribbon or lace to the ends of the scarf.

MATERIALS:

plain T-shirt (adult large
  or extra large)
8 inch (20.3 cm)
  paper plate
scissors

split key ring paper tags
small pictures
decoupage glue
paintbrush
pencil

Neck CHARMER

Ordinary becomes extraordinary as you transform a T-shirt and office supplies into a personalized fashion statement. Add scarf charms showcasing your interests.

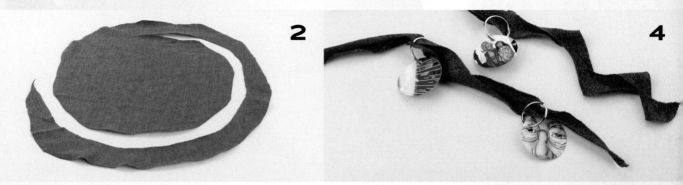

FOR THE SCARF:

1. Lay T-shirt flat. Use the paper plate as a tracing template to cut out as many circles as you can. Save the sleeves.

2. Turn a T-shirt circle into a spiral by cutting into the outside edge. Slowly curve the cuts inward until you reach the circle's center. You should have a long, spiraled strip of fabric. The more narrow the strip is cut, the longer the strand will be.

3. Repeat with each circle, cutting strips in different widths for variety.

4. Arrange the spiral strips into a row. Trim a hemmed cuff from the shirt sleeve and tie the cuff around the strips in the middle.

FOR THE CHARMS:

1. Remove the wire ring from the tags. Trim your picture to fit the tag circle.

2. Brush decoupage glue onto the tag. Attach the image and brush another layer of glue over the top. Let dry.

3. Turn the tag over and repeat step 2.

4. Use a pencil to poke a small hole in the key tag. Reattach the wire ring. Slide fabric between the key tag rings.

Tip: Print photos in the size you need, or look through magazines to find small pictures to use.

Funky FELTING

Re-use old sweaters to experiment with color blocking!
Create a fun geometric look that will have you looking
forward to a frosty forecast.

MATERIALS:
old woolen sweaters
  in various colors
netted laundry bag
scissors
needle and thread

*Tip: Not into squares or hexagons? Make
stencils in the shapes of quatrefoils,
chevrons, or any other fun design. Sew on
beads or jewels for some sparkle.*

1. Felt the sweaters first so they won't unravel. Put them in a netted bag and wash in hot water (no detergent needed). Spread the wet sweaters flat on towels to air dry.

2. Cut a scarf piece from one of the sweaters. Cut from a bottom hem over the sweater's shoulders to the hem on the other side of the sweater. Or you can cut around the sweater's torso in a spiral shape.

3. Cut out pieces of various shapes from the other sweaters. Squares, triangles, and hexagons are a few ideas. Cut additional smaller pieces in those same shapes, varying colors and tones.

4. Stitch the layered pieces together, starting with the largest and working your way to the smallest.

5. Sew the felt pieces onto the scarf.

Shimmering SHAWL

A chilly night calls for a lightweight wrap. Delicate tulle flowers turn flowy fabric into a shawl that's both pretty and practical.

MATERIALS:

lightweight fabric
scissors
needle and thread
3 inch (7.6 cm) circle stencil

burgundy tulle
gold tulle
buttons or beads
fabric glue

1. Cut fabric 32 by 50 inches (81.3 by 127 cm) to make the shawl. Hem the sides using a small straight stitch.

2. Use the stencil to cut out 24 circles from the burgundy tulle. Cut out 12 circles from the gold tulle.

3. Layer two burgundy circles on top of one gold circle. Pinch in the middle to create a flower shape. Whip stitch the pinched bottom section together. Use your fingers to flatten and shape the flower.

4. Repeat step 3 to make 12 flowers.

5. Glue beads or buttons to the center of each flower. Let dry.

6. Attach flowers along the edges of the shawl with the fabric glue. Add small stitches to reinforce, if desired.

Tip: Make as many or as few flowers as you want. A shawl covered with hundreds of flowers would make a huge impact!

Gauzy GLAM

Dream up a fanciful, lightweight summer covering with cheesecloth and fabric dye. Use an ombré technique to produce a gradual color shift from light to dark.

MATERIALS:

cheesecloth
scissors
hanger
drop cloth or old newspaper
small spray bottle
fabric dye
salt

Tip: Adding salt to the dye helps to keep the scarf's colors from washing away or getting onto other clothes. Handwashing is best, but use a delicate cycle if you toss it in the wash.

1. Cut a piece of cheesecloth about 14 by 63 inches (35.6 by 160 cm). Drape it on a hanger and carefully place it on the drop cloth.

2. Mix two capfuls of liquid dye and one tablespoon (14.8 milliliters) of salt in the spray bottle. Fill the rest of the way with hot water.

3. To create an ombré pattern, spritz the fabric from several inches away for the sections where you want a lighter color. Move closer and spray more heavily to make the color gradually darker. The fabric should be soaked, especially where you want the heaviest shade.

4. Let the scarf air dry on the drop cloth until it is slightly damp. Hang it up to finish drying.

MATERIALS:

flannel shirt with chest pockets (adult size)
scissors
sewing needle and thread
lace or trim

Comfy CARGO

On the go but no place to store your stuff? Turn an old flannel shirt into a handy scarf. The four pockets are tailor-made for weekend outings.

7

Tip: Chambray or corduroy shirts also work well for this project.

1. Cut out the front and back sections of the flannel shirt. Remove the chest pockets without cutting into the front section of the shirt.

2. Fold the back section in half lengthwise. Cut along the fold. Trim off any curved parts to make straight edges.

3. Put right sides together and stitch short edges to create a long scarf.

4. Cut the shirt's front to create two large pockets that are 12 inches (30.5 cm) long and as wide as the scarf.

5. Use a straight stitch to sew the small chest pockets onto the top middle of each large pocket section.

6. Pin and sew the large pocket sections to the back side of the scarf's bottom edges, using a whip stitch. Turn out the pockets so the seams are on the inside and the pockets now show on the scarf's front.

7. Fold the unfinished long edges of the scarf underneath twice and hem.

8. Sew lace or trim along the top edges of the large pockets.

MATERIALS:

decorative paper
scissors
ruler
glue stick
skewer

colored ribbons
yarn
binder clip
needle and thread

Edgy BOHO

From long skirts to beaded bangles, boho style
is here to stay. Create your own whimsical look
with a colorful scarf that's all your own.

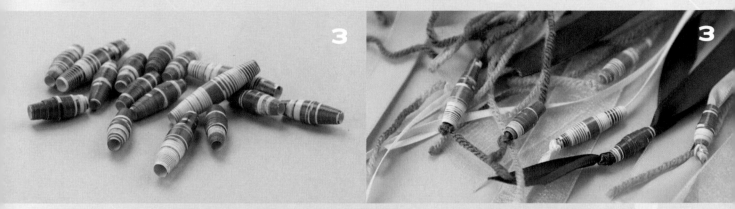

FOR THE BEADS:

1. Cut a triangle from the paper 10 inches (25.4 cm) long and 1 inch (2.5 cm) across at its widest point.

2. Lay triangle flat, pattern side down. Apply glue to the back.

3. Starting with the widest end, roll the paper around the skewer to make a bead. Slide the paper bead off the skewer to dry.

4. Repeat steps 1–3 to make 16 beads.

FOR THE SCARF:

1. Cut ribbons and yarn into 60 inch (152.4 cm) pieces. Arrange strands to form your scarf. Use a binder clip to hold the strips place.

2. Use needle and thread to tie the ribbons and yarn together in the center.

3. String beads onto the ribbons and yarn, knotting the ends to keep the beads from sliding off.

Tip: Create a little extra sparkle by adding glitter or
glow-in-the-dark craft paint to your beads. Make a few
extra beads to create a matching necklace or bracelet.

MATERIALS:

plain canvas bag
fabric
fabric scissors
pins

1-inch- (2.5-cm-) wide
grosgrain ribbon
fabric glue
fabric flower (optional)

Fun Ruffle TOTE

Need a tote to hold your gear? Don't get ruffled. (Or do!)
Fill your frilly tote and you're on your way wherever.

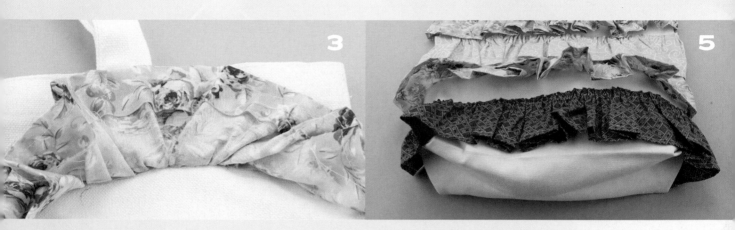

1. Measure the opening of the bag. Multiply by 3. Cut a strip of 4-inch- (10.2-cm-) wide fabric to this length. Sew the two short ends together to form a circular strip.

2. Fold under one long edge ¼ inch (0.6 cm) toward the wrong side. Fold over again and stitch in place.

3. Sew a basting stitch ¼ inch from the other long edge. Repeat ½ inch (1.3 cm) from the edge.

4. Pin the strip evenly around the top of the bag, with the raw edge one inch from the top. Pull the ends of the two top basting threads to make the fabric gather into a ruffle.

5. Sew the ruffle in place along the basting threads.

Tip: When cutting fabric, a fabric scissors (or shears) is best. A scissors made for cutting paper won't work as well. A regular scissors has handles that are the same size. On a fabric scissors, one handle is often much larger than the other. This allows you to hold the scissors with several fingers in the handle. Additionally, a fabric scissors is much sharper and able to easily cut through thick material.

scissors
fabric with large,
   simple designs
vinyl zipper wallet
fabric decoupage glue
   and foam brush

clear acrylic spray sealant
4mm to 6mm glass beads
head pin
pliers
6mm split ring

Decoupage WALLET

*For occasions that don't call for a big purse, a
super cute wallet is just the thing. Don't search
everywhere for that special, just-your-style wallet.
Do it yourself with decoupage!*

7

*Tip: Find cool designs on vintage
clothes or pillowcases at yard
sales and thrift shops.*

1. Cut out the designs from the fabric. Cover the wallet with decoupage glue and press the fabric onto the wallet. Let dry.

2. Cover the wallet with another coat of decoupage glue. Repeat for a glossier look.

3. When the decoupage is completely dry, spray the wallet with acrylic sealant.

4. For the zipper pull, arrange the beads on a head pin. Leave ½ inch of wire at the top.

5. Use pliers to twist the end of the head pin into a loop.

6. Attach a split ring to the loop.

7. Use the split ring to connect the beaded pull to the zipper.

Glam-Handle PURSE

Got an old purse with worn-out handles? Don't just toss it! Dress it up with a trendy new handle made of gold chain and colorful leather.

MATERIALS:

wire cutter
purse with damaged handles, connected with metal rings
6 feet (1.8 m) of 10-mm by 7-mm chain
24 feet (7.3 m) of 3-mm suede lace
hot glue and hot glue gun
4 jump rings
round-nosed jewelry pliers

1. Use the wire cutter to remove the purse's handles. Cut four lengths of chain the same length as the old handles.

2. Cut two pieces of suede lace that are 3 times the length of one chain.

3. Lay two chains side-by-side and thread a piece of lace through the top rings.

4. Wrap the ends of the lace under the chains and through the next chain link. Cross the lace and weave it through the next chain link. Continue weaving over and under so that the laces form X's that join the two chains together.

5. At the end of the chain, knot and trim the lace. Glue the ends down with hot glue.

6. Use the jump rings to attach the handle to the purse.

7. Repeat steps 3–6 to make a second handle.

Tip: Craft and discount stores sell inexpensive jewelry starter kits that include wire cutters, round-nosed pliers, and an assortment of head pins and jump rings.

MATERIALS:

medium-sized canvas tote
½ yard (½ m) print fabric
iron
pins
needle and thread or sewing machine
ribbon trim with tassels

Pocket TOTE

A crafty girl just can't have enough totes. Whatever your hobby—sewing, beading, painting—you need to keep your supplies together while you're at home. This tote looks pretty while it keeps your project organized and portable.

FOR THE HANDLES:

1. Measure one of the bag's handles. Add 1 inch (2.5 cm) to the width and length. Cut a length of fabric to this size.

2. Fold the sides of the fabric under ½ inch (1.3 cm) and iron in place. Pin the folds to the handle. Sew along each edge. Repeat for the second handle.

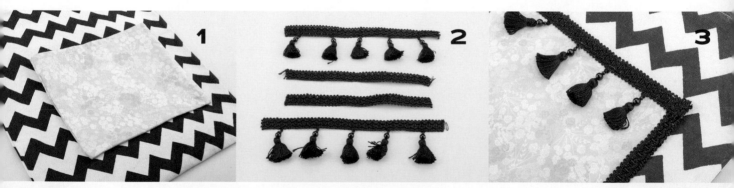

FOR THE POCKET:

1. Cut a piece of fabric 8 by 11 inches (20.3 by 28 cm). Place the fabric on the tote as desired. Sew the two sides and the bottom of the fabric to the tote to make a pocket.

2. Measure and cut the ribbon into four pieces long enough to trim the fabric pocket.

3. Sew or glue the ribbon along the outside of the fabric. (Be sure not to sew the pocket shut.) Trim the tassels from the side pieces of trim, if desired.

Tip: Tassels not your thing? Make a monogram with black buttons on the pocket instead.

Super Sleepover SACK

Start with some pretty fabric, satin ribbon, and a few seams. End up with a cute drawstring bag to hold your pajamas and toiletries. Your friends won't believe you made it!

MATERIALS:

½ yard (½ m) of cotton fabric
iron
needle and thread or sewing machine
pins
safety pin
1 yard (0.9 m) white satin ribbon, ¾ inch
    (1.9 cm) wide

Tip: The selvage edge of fabric is finished by the manufacturer so it won't ravel. Selvages should be trimmed away before you begin a project because they are thicker than the rest of the fabric.

1. Trim off 2 inches (5 cm) of the selvage side of the fabric.

2. Hem one long raw edge of the fabric by folding it in ½ inch (1.3 cm), ironing, and sewing in place.

3. Fold the fabric in half vertically. On the wrong side of the fabric, sew a ½-inch (1.3-cm) seam across the bottom and up the side. Stop 4 inches (10.2 cm) before the top edge. Backstitch.

4. Fold the top edge down 2 inches (5.1 cm). Pin. Sew close to the top edge and along the lower edge to form a casing.

5. Turn the bag right-side-out. Attach a safety pin to the end of the ribbon. Push the closed safety pin into the casing and feed the ribbon through to the other side. Remove the safety pin, and tie the ends of the ribbon in a knot.

MATERIALS:
two coordinated pillowcases
measuring tape
scissors
needle and thread or
   sewing machine
pins

Pillowy PURSE

If you and your best friend like do-it-yourself projects, this one's for you! With just a few simple steps, you'll have matching bags to carry your stuff everywhere.

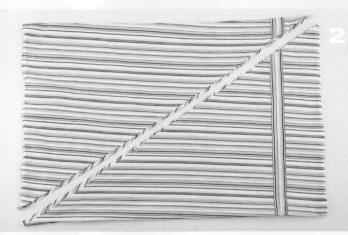

1. Trim ¼ inch (0.6 cm) off the closed end of each pillowcase.

2. Cut each case in half diagonally the long way.

3. Turn under the diagonal cut edges ¼ inch and sew to make a narrow hem.

4. Place one pillowcase half inside the other half and line up the bottom edges. Pin and sew where the fabrics overlap in front, being careful not to sew through the back.

5. Repeat step 4 on the back side.

6. Turn the fabric inside out and sew the bottom onto the other half of the pillowcase.

7. Turn the purse right-side-out and tie the top ends with a knot to make a handle.

Tip: Pillowcases make great totes for books, sports equipment, or hobby supplies. If they get dirty, you can just toss them in the washing machine.

Monogram Glitter
WRISTLET

Every girl needs a sparkly wristlet to hold a few dollars or an ID card. Skip the pricey boutique and make your own. Use the cuff of a shirt that's on its way to the thrift shop.

MATERIALS:

scissors
old long-sleeve dress shirt
ribbon
needle and thread
   or sewing machine

seam ripper
button
washable marker
fabric glitter glue
glitter

1. Cut the cuff off the sleeve.

2. Cut 10 inches (25.4 cm) of ribbon. Fold the ribbon in half to form a wrist loop. Insert the two raw edges into the side of the cuff about 1 inch (2.5 cm) below the button.

3. With the flap open, sew along the sides of the cuff to form a pocket.

4. Use a seam ripper to remove the old button. Replace with a fun, colorful button.

5. With the cuff buttoned, use a light washable marker to draw the shape of your initial.

6. Fill the initial with glue and sprinkle on glitter. Gently shake off extra glitter. Dry completely before using.

Tip: When throwing away damaged clothing, use a seam ripper to take off fancy buttons. Save them in a jar so you'll be ready for projects like this one.

Beautiful Bow BAG

Start with a blanket and end up with a soft bag! Fill it with pajamas, swimming supplies, or gym clothes.

1. Fold the blanket in half. Fold it in half again so that you have a corner and four layers.

2. Holding the start of the measuring tape at the corner of the blanket, make marks at the 14-inch (35.6 cm) point every 2 inches (5.1 cm). Connect the marks to make an arc. Cut along the marks. Unfold.

3. With the circle folded in half, mark thirteen 1-inch (2.5-cm) lines. Make them about 3 inches (7.6 cm) apart and 1.5 inches (3.8 cm) from the edge. Cut through both sides. Open.

4. Cut the ribbon into two 1-yard (0.9-m) lengths.

5. Sew the ends of one ribbon to opposite sides of the circle. Center each end between two slits. This will be the handle.

6. Thread the other ribbon in and out of the slits. Pull the ends to gather and close the purse. Tie a bow.

Tip: Fleece is easy to work with because it doesn't ravel. Dollar and discount stores carry inexpensive fleece blankets. Or you could buy fleece material at a fabric store.

MATERIALS:

scissors
sequined fabric
lining fabric
lightweight fusible
  interfacing
washcloth
iron

needle and thread or
  sewing machine
½-inch- (1.3-cm-)
  wide ribbon
hot glue and hot
  glue gun
3 hook and loop fasteners
  with adhesive backs

Sparkly Bow CLUTCH

Going to a fancy party? You'll look great carrying this shiny little bag! Slide your hand under the bow to hold it.

1. Cut a 10-by-9 inch (25.4-by-23 cm) rectangle from the sequined fabric. Cut a 10-by-18-inch (25.4-by-45.7-cm) rectangle from the sequined fabric, the lining fabric, and the interfacing.

2. Place the interfacing on the wrong side of the larger sequined fabric rectangle. The fusible side of the interfacing should face down. Set the washcloth on top of the interfacing to protect the sequins. With the iron set on low, gently fuse interfacing to the wrong side of the sequined fabric.

3. Sew the larger sequin rectangle and the lining together with right sides facing in. Leave a 3-inch (7.6-cm) opening along one side. Turn right-side-out. Set the iron to low and press the lining side gently.

4. Fold the fabric from step 3 into thirds with the sequined side out. Sew along the sides to form a pocket.

5. Fold the smaller sequined fabric rectangle in half lengthwise, right-side-in. Sew along the edges, leaving a 3-inch (7.6-cm) opening. Turn right-side-out. Press open with your fingers or cover with a washcloth and press with the iron set on low.

6. Sew the short ends of the smaller rectangle to the sides of the flap from step 4.

7. Cut a 4-inch (10.2-cm) length of ribbon. Pleat the center of the smaller rectangle and wrap the ribbon around the pleat to hold in place. Use hot glue to secure the ribbon.

8. Attach the adhesive circles to the center and corners of the underside of the flap. Attach the other halves to the center and corners of the front of the pocket.

INTERFACING

Interfacing makes fabric stiffer and thicker. Fusible interfacing has a rough side that fuses or sticks to fabric when it's ironed. To apply, place the bumpy side of the interfacing against the wrong side of the fabric, cover with a damp washcloth, and press for 10 to 15 seconds. Pick up the iron and repeat until you've covered the entire piece.

Wacky, Woolly WALLET

The wallet is the heart of a purse. It keeps your cards and money safe and organized. Choose felt in wild colors for this bifold bag so you can find it fast.

1. Cut rectangles from the felt in the following sizes:
   - outer piece: one 4-by-7-inch (10.2-by-17.8-cm) piece
   - inner piece: one 3 ¾-by-7-inch (9.5-by-17.8-cm) piece
   - pockets: four 3 ¾-by-2 ¼-inch (9.5-by-5.7-cm) pieces
   - tab: one 2 ¾-by-2 ½-inch (7-by-6.4-cm) piece

2. Pin one pocket piece on the inner piece ½ inch (1.3 cm) from the top. Sew the sides and bottom edge.

3. Overlap the next pocket piece ½ inch (1.3 cm) from the top of the first pocket. Sew in place along the sides and bottom edge.

4. Sew the outer piece to the inner piece, tucking the end of the tab in the middle of one side. Sew on the sides and bottom edge.

5. Attach the hook and loop fasteners to the underside of the tab and the outside of the wallet.

6. Hot glue ribbon to the outside edges. Sew a button to the outside of the tab.

Tip: For a more sophisticated look, use neutral colors such as black or gray. Decorate the wallet and tab with strips of beaded trim instead of ribbons and a button.

MATERIALS:

scissors
cotton fabric in two patterns
   (one for pouch, one for lining)
¼-yard (0.2-m) lightweight
   fusible interfacing
drinking glass
pencil
iron
44 inches (111.8 cm) of
   1-inch- (2.5-cm-) wide cotton
   twill tape
large eyelet kit
hook and loop fasteners with
   adhesive backs
½-inch (1.3-cm) swivel hook

Cell Phone POCKET

Are you lost without your cell phone? Never feel that way again with this lightweight, hands-free holder.

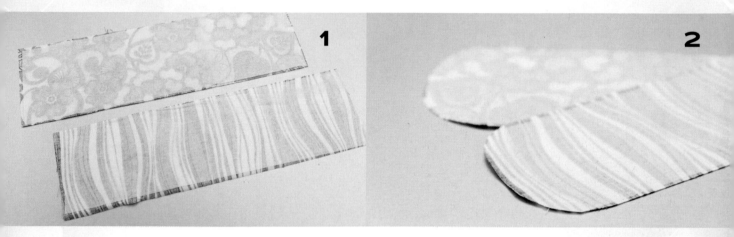

1. Cut a 4-by-14-inch (10.2-by-35.6-cm) rectangle from each fabric. Cut a same-size rectangle from the interfacing.

2. Use an upside-down drinking glass to trace and cut a rounded end on each of the fabric pieces.

3. Follow the instructions on the package to fuse the interface to the wrong side of the lining.

4. Pin the pouch and lining together, right-side-in. Sew around the edge in a ¼-inch (0.6-cm) seam, leaving a 2-inch (5.1-cm) opening on the left side.

5. Trim the corners, clip the curves, and turn right-side-out. Iron.

6. Fold the pouch so that 1 inch (2.5 cm) of the curved ends makes a flap. This is where the eyelet will go. Line up the hook and loop pieces on the inside lining and stick on.

continued on next page

9

11

7. Fold the pouch and stitch along the edges.

8. Follow the instructions on the eyelet kit to apply the eyelet to the center of the flap.

9. Fold the twill tape in half lengthwise. Sew along both long edges, stitching ⅛ inch (0.3 cm) from the edge.

10. Slide the swivel hook into the strap and line up the two raw edges. Sew two or three times in a ½-inch (1.3-cm) seam. Trim the seam allowances.

11. Flip the strap so the seam is on the inside. Slide the hook down so it rests at the sewn end. Sew across the strap just above the hook to hold in place.

12. Attach the strap to the eyelet.

Tip: If you are short on interfacing, it's okay to press pieces side-by-side. Just don't overlap them or they'll make a bump in your finished piece.

MATERIALS:

- marker
- 3.5 inch (8.9 cm) sew-in purse frame
- paper
- scraps of fabric
- lining fabric
- fusible interfacing
- iron
- damp cloth
- needle and thread or sewing machine

Sweet Coin KEEPER

Coins rattling around in the bottom of your bag? This project's for you! Use a sew-in clasp to make this clever little purse.

1

Tip: Sew-in or glue-in metal purse frames are sold at craft and fabric stores.

1. To make a pattern, lay the purse frame on a sheet of plain paper and trace around the outside edge of the frame, skipping the clasp. Then draw out from the clasp's hinge to freehand the shape of your purse. Add ¼ inch for the seam allowance.

2. Use the pattern to cut out two purse pieces, two lining pieces, and two pieces of fusible interfacing. Mark the fabric pieces with dots to show where the hinge will be on each side. Flip the pattern over to be sure everything is even. Otherwise you may end up with mismatched edges.

3. Using the damp cloth, fuse the interfacing to the wrong side of the purse pieces.

4. With the right sides together, sew the purse pieces together. Stop at the dots that mark the hinges. Repeat for the lining sections.

5. Turn the purse right-side-out. Push the lining into the purse and iron together.

6. Stitch the lining and purse together around the top edge with a ⅛-inch (0.3-cm) seam.

7. Push the edge of the purse into the frame and stitch in place.

MATERIALS:

old hardback book
utility knife
fabric for lining
scissors
pencil
iron

1-inch (2.5-cm-) wide
   heavyweight ribbon
wooden purse handles
needle and thread or sewing
   machine
hot glue and hot glue gun
decorative flower (optional)

Book BAG

Find an old hardback book on a library give-away shelf or at a yard sale. Add some trendy fabric and wooden handles and transform a worn-out book into a stylish purse.

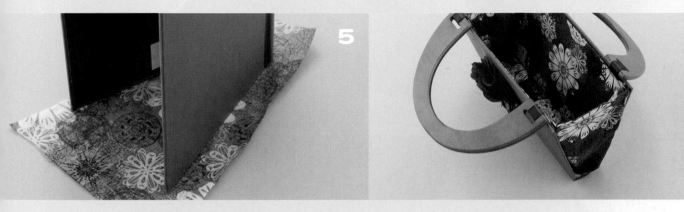

1. Use a utility knife to cut the pages from the book, leaving the cover and spine.

2. Use the open book cover to trace and cut a piece of fabric the same size. Fold and iron the edges of the fabric in ½-inch (1.3-cm) from the outside.

3. Cut four 5-inch (12.7-cm) lengths of ribbon. Thread one ribbon end through the hole in the base of the purse handle. Sew the raw edges of the ribbon together. Repeat with the other three ribbons.

4. Line the handles up with the edges of the book cover. Glue the ribbons to the inside of the cover.

5. Set the open book upright on a large piece of paper. Draw a line from the edges of the spine out to make a triangle. This will be the pattern for the sides of the purse. Add ¼-inch (0.6-cm) to the outside of the pattern for the seam allowance, and an inch to the height at the narrow end. Use this pattern to cut four pieces of fabric for the purse sides.

6. Sew the pairs of purse sides, right sides together, leaving a 2-inch (5.1-cm) opening. Turn and press. Hot glue the triangles to the purse sides. Hot glue the rectangle from step 2 to the inside of the book cover.

Tip: You can find purse handles at discount, craft, and fabric stores. Choose from bamboo, leather, or colored vinyl.

MATERIALS:

two kitchen or tea towels
scissors
patterned felt
pins
needle and thread or
   sewing machine
iron-on embellishments

flat-backed jewels
craft glue
2-inch- (5.1-cm-) wide
   cotton twill tape
   or webbing
iron

Trendy Towel TOTE

Pretty kitchen towels are not just for drying dishes! Show off your sewing skills by turning a pair of towels into a terrific handbag. When you see how quick and easy it is, you're going to want more than one!

1. Trim away the hemmed edges of the towels. If needed, trim the towels to the same size.

2. Cut around the patterns on the felt, or freehand your own. Pin them to the right side of one of the tea towels.

3. Sew the felt shapes to the towel.

4. Iron on the embellishments and glue on the jewels.

5. Fold the appliquéd towel in half, right-side-in, to form a bag. Sew the sides and bottom together. Repeat for the second towel.

6. Turn the outer bag (the one with the appliqués) so it's right-side-out. Turn the raw edge of the bag under ½ inch (1.3 cm) and iron. Repeat for the second bag.

7. Slip the lining bag into the outer bag. Pin the edges together. Sew.

8. Cut two 19-inch (48.3-cm) lengths of twill tape. Sew in place for handles.

Tips: Medium-weight cotton towels work best for this project. Avoid terrycloth. Its thickness and texture make it difficult to sew.

To reinforce the handles, sew a square at the base, going through both the handle and the bag. Sew an X inside each square.

MATERIALS:

9 inch (22.9 cm) nylon zipper
two 9-by-7-inch (22.9-by-17.8-cm) pieces of cotton fabric, for lining

two 9-by-7-inch (22.9-by-17.8-cm) pieces of cotton fabric, for pouch
pins
sewing machine

Zippy Pencil POUCH

Sew up this handy little bag in a sec. Then fill it with your favorite pencils and throw it in your backpack with a sketchpad.

1. Place the wrong side of the zipper along the long top edge of the lining fabric. Make sure the zipper touches the right side of the fabric. Place the pouch fabric over the zipper, right-side-down. Use pins to hold the zipper in place.

2. Stitch the zipper and material in place. Use a zipper foot, if you're using a sewing machine.

3. Fold the pouch and lining fabrics away from the zipper

4. Repeat steps 1 and 3 on the other side of the zipper.

5. Topstitch along the edges of the fabric, close to the zipper.

6. Open the zipper about two-thirds of the way. (If you don't open the zipper, you won't be able to turn the pouch right-side-out after it's sewn.) Place the pouch and lining fabrics right sides together. Fold the zipper teeth toward the lining. Pin.

7. Sew around the edges of the pouch and lining with a ½-inch (1.3-cm) seam, leaving a 3 inch (7.6 cm) opening on the bottom edge of the lining. Clip corners and turn right-side-out.

8. Topstitch the opening in the bottom of the lining. Push the lining into the pouch and zip it up!

Tip: A zipper foot is different from the all-purpose foot used for regular machine sewing. It's thinner and has a notch for the needle. This lets you sew close to the edge of the zipper.

CLIPPING CURVES

To make rounded corners lay flat, make slits perpendicular to the stitches every ½-inch (1.3-cm) around the curve before you turn your project right-side-out. Be careful not to clip the stitches!

Rock a Color BLOCK

What says "happy" better than a pop of color? This dressed-up bag is the perfect way to jazz up a standard leggings-and-tee combo.

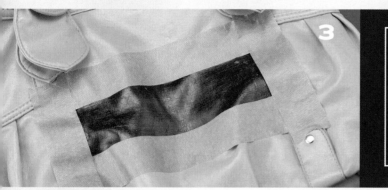

Tip: For maximum flair, choose bright, contrasting colors like purple and orange or turquoise and yellow.

1. Sand the section of the leather purse you would like to paint. The surface needs to be rough so the paint will stick.

2. Wipe the purse with a clean cloth to remove any residue. Wipe again with a cloth dampened with rubbing alcohol.

3. Mask the edges of the sanded section with painter's tape.

4. Use a mixture of half paint and half water to paint the section.

5. When the section is almost dry, apply a second coat.

6. Continue steps 4 and 5 until you are happy with the color. Let dry, then remove tape.

7. Use sticky-back jewels and embellishments to decorate the purse.

8. Spray the entire purse with an acrylic sealant. Let dry before using.

Denim DELIGHT

Do you have an old pair of jeans with grass stains and ripped holes? Or perhaps you have outgrown a comfy fleece or favorite tee. Think twice before you throw them away. Instead, make a stylish bracelet in minutes.

MATERIALS:

scissors	end caps
old jeans, fleece, or T-shirt	chain
	jump rings
thread	lobster clasp
fabric glue	round-nosed pliers

1. Cut fabric into three pieces, each 10 inches (25.4 cm) long by 1 inch (2.5 cm) wide.

2. Secure the pieces together by wrapping one end with a 10-inch (25.4-cm) piece of thread. Wrap the thread around the fabric ends 20 times, and then knot the thread to hold it in place.

3. Braid the fabric pieces, leaving a 1-inch (2.5-cm) tail.

4. Repeat step 2 at the other end of the braid.

5. After both ends are tied off with thread, use the scissors to trim off the extra fabric.

6. Dab some fabric glue in an end cap. Insert one end of the braid into the cap. Repeat on the other end. Let dry.

7. Wrap a chain around the length of the bracelet. Use jump rings to connect the ends of the chain to the end caps.

8. Attach the lobster clasp to the end caps using round-nosed pliers.

Tip: The wider you cut the fabric, the thicker the bracelet will be. Thinner fabric will make for a smaller, daintier bracelet.

MATERIALS:
20-gauge wire
wire cutter
round-nosed pliers
small beads
ball pins
large charm (optional)

Open-Ended WIRE WRAP

A wire wrap is the perfect statement piece that's casual enough for school. Get fancy with pearls and crystals, or keep it casual with glass and metal beads.

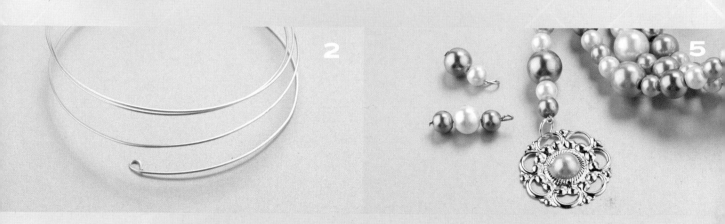

1. Wrap the wire around your wrist 3 to 5 times, and cut the end.

2. Use the pliers to bend one end of the wire into a tiny loop to stop the beads from falling off. The loop also creates a place to connect charms.

3. Thread beads onto the wire until covered.

4. Bend another tiny loop on the other end to prevent the beads from falling off.

5. Create charms by threading one to three beads onto a ball pin. To finish the charm, bend a loop with the end of the ball pin wire and wrap the tail around itself. If the tail is too long, trim it with the wire cutter.

6. Attach charms to both loop ends of the bracelet. You can also add the large charm, if desired.

Tip: Maintain a minimalist look with beads in all one color or style. Or go bold with a fun pattern of brightly-colored beads.

MATERIALS:

scissors
1-inch- (2.5-cm-) wide ribbon
buttons
needle and thread (optional)

Button NECKLACE

If you enjoy sewing in your free time, this bracelet is for you! Put your crafty talents to work by sewing colorful buttons onto ribbon to make a uniquely styled bracelet.

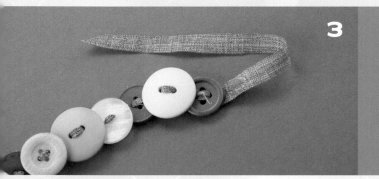

3

> Tips: Cover buttons with fabric or scrapbook paper and decoupage glue. Layer small buttons over larger buttons, or decorate with glitter.

1. Cut the ribbon to your desired necklace length.

2. Lay the buttons alongside the ribbon in the desired pattern.

3. Thread the ribbon through the buttons. (If the button holes are too small, use a needle and thread to weave the buttons onto the ribbon.)

4. Adjust the buttons so they are centered on the ribbon. Then knot the ends of the ribbon to keep the buttons in place.

5. Cut two 4-inch- (10.2-cm-) long pieces of ribbon. Tie one in a bow around one of the knots you tied in step 4. Repeat on the other side of the necklace.

MATERIALS:

small round beads
eye pins
round-nosed pliers
16-gauge wire

wire cutter
small square jump rings
small round jump rings

Caged Bead
CHARM BRACELET

Get up close and personal with caged beads. Create your own charms using fancy caging techniques, beads, and tiny trinkets.

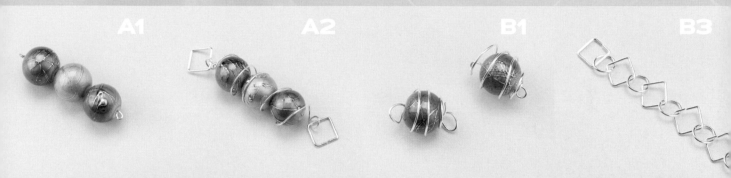

A1 **A2** **B1** **B3**

FOR STYLE A:

1. Thread three beads onto the eye pin.

2. Use the round-nosed pliers to bend a closed loop in the top of your eye pin, wrapping the extra wire around itself.

3. Coil wire around the beads. Wrap one end around the eye pin loop. Twist the other end of the wire to create a loop at the bottom of the beads.

FOR STYLE B:

1. Cut a 2-inch (5.1-cm) piece of wire. Shape the top part in a tight coil, and then do the same with the bottom piece but in the opposite direction to create an "S" shape with the wire.

2. Slip the bead or trinket in the middle and pull the coil over it to enclose it. Create a loop with the wire on one end to attach to a jump ring. Cut off any excess wire.

3. Use jump rings like bracelet links, attaching the charms to each other.

Tip: For a different look, change up the finish of the wire. Try gold, antiqued, or colored metal.

MATERIALS:

scissors
2mm leather cording
button
seed beads
small jump rings

Stylish Seed BEADS

Sometimes store-bought presents just won't do for the special person in your life. Instead, surprise them with this long-lasting leather bracelet. It's a gift your friend can treasure forever.

1. Cut a piece of leather cording 15 inches (38.1 cm) long.

2. Thread the button onto the cording and tie a knot to keep it at the center of the cord.

3. Place two seed beads on one half of the cording and one seed bead on the other half.

4. Thread two jump rings over both pieces of cording until they hit the bottom of the beads. Place two seed beads on the piece with one bead, and one seed bead on the cord with two beads.

5. Thread two more jump rings over the cording. Repeat this pattern until most of the cording has been covered.

6. Knot the two pieces of cording together. Leave ½ inch (1.3 cm) space and tie a second knot to create a hook for the button clasp. Trim off any extra cording.

Tip: Replace the leather cording with embroidery floss or wire. Make a few bracelets and wear them stacked together!

Triple Strand DELIGHT

Accessorizing accents in groups of threes or fives draws the eye and shows off your style. A simple way to achieve this look is with the Triple Strand Delight. Bead three bracelets in three different styles, then connect them onto one clasp to create a 3-in-1 beauty!

MATERIALS:

embroidery floss
scissors
beads in three styles
jump rings

round-nosed pliers
crimp end caps
 with loops
clasp

Tip: Use similarly colored beads and floss to create a uniform look, or get colorful by using different colored beads and floss for each strand.

1. Wrap embroidery floss around your wrist. Add 1 inch (2.5 cm) and cut. Repeat this step two more times.

2. Tie the three pieces of embroidery floss together at one end, leaving a ½ inch (1.3 cm) tail.

3. Decorate one strand with all the beads touching each other. Knot the end to keep beads in place.

4. Bead the next strand with the second type of bead. Add a knot between each bead, then make a final knot at the end.

5. Bead the last strand with a third type of bead. Spread out your knots to create a strand with even fewer beads. Make a final knot at the end. Then tie the ends of all three strands together, leaving a ½ inch (1.3 cm) tail.

6. Use the pliers to crimp an end cap at both ends of the bracelet.

7. Connect the clasp to one end cap using jump rings.

Wire and Bead BANGLE

Wire creates a modern look, but adding curls and twists softens the vibe. Try stacking a few color-coordinated bangles for added dimension.

MATERIALS:

wire cutter
24-gauge wire
round-nosed pliers
beads
14-gauge wire

Tip: Use similar steps to make matching rings, earrings, and necklaces.

1. Cut the 24-gauge wire to the desired bracelet length (once around your wrist). Add an extra ¼ inch (0.6 cm) for the looped ends.

2. Use the pliers to bend one end into a small loop.

3. Thread beads onto the bracelet until all but the last inch is decorated. Bend the other end of the wire into a loop to keep the beads from falling off.

4. Tightly wrap the 14-gauge wire around one end of the bracelet several times until you reach the first bead. Cover the end of the thin wire as you wrap.

5. Wrap the wire between and around the beads until you reach the other end of the bracelet. Cut the wire, then tuck the end under the wraps.

Lacy WRISTLET

This bracelet is elegant and whimsical. Practice your sewing skills as you create this beauty. Plan to use lace and beads all in the same color, or get imaginative mixing different shades.

MATERIALS:

wide, heavy lace
needle and thread
pearl and crystal beads
ribbon

Tip: Use pearl and crystal beads to make this elegant bracelet. For an everyday look, use glass or metal beads.

1. Measure and cut the lace to fit around your wrist.

2. Start at one end of the lace and begin sewing the beads along the pattern of the lace. Continue until the lace is covered with the desired number of beads.

3. Cut two 5 inch (12.7 cm) pieces of ribbon. Use the needle and thread to sew one ribbon to one end of the bracelet. Repeat on the other side with the second ribbon.

4. Secure the bracelet onto your wrist using the ribbon to tie a bow.

Friendship STACKS

For a spin on the classic friendship bracelet, consider a friendship anklet instead. Design your anklets to either match or complement each other. You can even make them in a few different colors to go with everything in your wardrobe.

MATERIALS:

colored hemp cording	end caps
metal ring	jump rings
fabric glue	lobster clasp

Tip: Save this project for your next sleepover. Then you and your friends can make them together.

1. Cut three pieces of cording 20 inches (50.8 cm) long.

2. Fold the cording in half and thread the folded portion through the metal ring. Feed the cording through the loop to secure it on the ring.

3. Braid one side of the cord until you reach the end of the cord.

4. Trim the ends of the cords to make them even. Glue the ends and push them into the end cap. Let dry.

5. Repeat steps 1–4 to add three more braided cords. You should have two cords on each side of the metal ring.

6. Use jump rings to attach clasps to the end caps.

Feathers and RIBBON

Channel your inner hippie with this whimsical look. Mixed textures add depth and complexity to any jewelry. Pick your favorite combinations of colored feathers and ribbon to make this unique trendsetter.

MATERIALS:

scissors
¼-inch- (0.6-cm-) wide ribbon
fabric glue
7 small feathers, about 1 inch (2.5 cm) long

1-inch (2.5-cm) fringe ribbon (optional)
ribbon clamps
round-nosed pliers
jump rings
clasp

Tip: If you can't find small feathers, simply cut longer feathers into 1-inch (2.5-cm) pieces. You can also make your own faux feathers using felt, suede, or other heavier fabrics. Use a stencil or create your own freehand style.

1. Cut two pieces of ribbon to fit around your shoe or boot.

2. Lay one piece of ribbon flat. Place dots of glue along the ribbon, each about ½ inch (1.3 cm) apart.

3. Place the ends of the small feathers or the fringe ribbon on the glue.

4. Squeeze a thin stripe of glue over the feathers. Press the second piece of ribbon on top of the first.

5. Attach a clamp to both ends of the ribbon. Secure with glue.

6. Use jump rings and round-nosed pliers to attach the clasp.

MATERIALS:
round-nosed pliers
jump rings
seed beads
lobster or toggle clasp

Jump Ring CHAIN

Did you ever make paper chain decorations when you were younger? Here's the bejeweled version. Instead of paper strips, use shiny metal rings and sparkling beads to make an ankle bracelet.

Tip: Jump rings are small metal rings used for crafting. They are sold in sizes between 2mm and 20mm and come in many different metals and finishes. Try making your own jump rings. Coil 16-gauge wire around a pen or pencil four or five times. Remove the coil and use a wire cutter to cut the rings.

1. Use the pliers to open a jump ring. Thread on two seed beads.

2. Close the jump ring to hold the beads in place.

3. Open the next jump ring and link it with the first jump ring. Close it without adding any beads.

4. Open another jump ring and thread on two beads. Hook it into the previous jump ring and squeeze it closed. Follow this with an empty jump ring.

5. Continue the pattern until you have reached the desired length.

6. Attach the clasp to the jump rings at both ends of your anklet.

Heart Wire and CRYSTALS

Give the special people in your life a homemade heart they can keep close.

Tip: Try bending shapes such as spirals, triangles, or ovals with your 24-gauge wire. Or bend the wire into cursive words, such as your name.

1. Cut a 3 inch (7.6 cm) piece of the 24-gauge wire. Use the pliers to bend it into a heart shape.

2. String a bead onto the heart. Loop the ends of the wire to close the heart.

3. Cut one 8-inch (20.3-cm) piece of the 16-gauge wire. Bend one end around the heart's wire.

4. String beads onto the 16-gauge wire, leaving a ¼-inch (0.6-cm) tail.

5. Close the 16-gauge wire around the other side of the heart.

Wire-Wrapped
BEAD RING

Sometimes the prettiest accessories are the simplest. With just three materials, you can make a beautiful ring for a fun night out.

MATERIALS:

24-gauge wire
wire cutter
small beads

Tip: Put on as many beads as you want. You can even go all the way around the ring with beads. If you choose to do this, make sure the beads are small to prevent the ring from feeling too bulky.

1. Wrap wire loosely around your finger five times to size your ring. Cut.

2. Cut a 4-inch (10.2-cm) piece of wire. String three beads onto the wire, leaving a ¼-inch (0.6-cm) tail at the end. Line the beads up on top of the ring.

3. Wrap the smaller piece of wire around the ring several times to cover the tail. Continue wrapping the wire around the ring, weaving between the beads to hold them in place.

4. When most of the wire is wrapped, tuck the tail into a section of wrapped wire.

MATERIALS:
22-gauge wire
wire cutter
round-nosed pliers
small jump rings
seed beads
ball pins

Simply CHARMING

*This tiny charm ring is another example of
simple elegance. Wear several at a time for a
statement piece that will draw the eye.*

1. Wrap the wire around your finger and cut to desired length, plus 1 inch (2.5 cm).

2. Use the pliers to shape little loops at each end of the wire. Hook the loops together to close the ring.

3. Repeat steps 1 and 2 to create a second and third ring. Use a jump ring to attach the rings' loops so instead of three small rings you have one large.

4. To make charms, thread one to three beads onto each ball pin. Bend a loop at the top and wrap the tail around the ball pin to keep the beads on the pin.

5. Repeat step 4 to create a second charm.

6. Attach the charms to the jump ring.

Tip: Small store-bought charms also work well.

MATERIALS:

wool roving
foam pad and
 felting needle

needle and thread
small gems or beads

Wild and WOOLLY

Here's a fun way to introduce new materials into your accessory stash. Soft, wool fiber makes these rings comfortable to wear on fingers or toes.

1

Tip: Sew just a few beads clustered together in one place, or space gems all around the outside of your ring.

1. Roll the wool roving between your fingers to create a tight, worm-shaped strand about 3 inches (7.6 cm) long.

2. Size the fiber around your finger, wrapping it around loosely a few times.

3. Continue to roll the looped fiber between your fingers until it stays together in a ring shape.

4. Place the fiber on the foam pad. Use the felting needle to poke the wool fiber multiple times until the wool fiber holds together tightly.

5. Start sewing from the inside of your ring outward, so the thread's knot is hidden. Sew tiny gems and beads to the outside of the ring.

Donut RING

Show off your tasteful fashion sense with a delicious donut ring.

MATERIALS:

light brown polymer clay
straw
pastel-colored polymer clay

liquid polymer clay
toothpick
craft knife
metal glue
metal ring base

2

1. Knead the clay in your hands until soft. Roll light brown clay into small balls. Flatten slightly.

2. Use a straw to make a hole in the middle of the ball. Smooth out the hole to make a donut shape.

3. In a small bowl, combine very small pieces of pastel-colored clay with a layer of liquid clay. Mix thoroughly until the pastel clay is liquefied.

4. Use a toothpick to dab the liquefied clay onto a donut to make icing.

5. Roll pieces of pastel clay very thin. Then cut tiny pieces with a craft knife to make sprinkles. You can also decorate your donuts with glitter or different colors of icing.

6. Bake donuts according to the instructions on the clay packet. Let cool completely before handling.

7. Use metal glue to attach a donut to a ring base. Let dry completely before wearing.

Tip: Tons of tiny food can be made from polymer clay! Ice cream cones, pretzels, cake, and fruit are only a few ideas. Make a cake or pizza, cut it into wedges, and turn each wedge into a bracelet charm. Give a piece to each of your friends. It's the ultimate friendship bracelet!

Woven RING

Spice up your party attire with this simple, yet memorable design. The ring is smooth and flat so it fits comfortably on your toe.

MATERIALS:

16-gauge wire
wire cutter
thin leather cording
fabric glue

Tip: If you don't have leather cording, you can weave other materials into your ring. Try making this ring with ribbon, wire, or embroidery floss.

1. Cut a 7-inch (17.8-cm) piece of wire. Bend the wire around your toe three times. Trim off any extra wire.

2. Cut a 10-inch (25.4-cm) piece of leather cording.

3. Use the basket weave technique to weave the cording all the way around the ring.

4. Once you reach your starting point, cut off any extra cording.

5. Use the fabric glue to hold the two cording ends together. Let the glue dry completely before wearing your ring.

HOW TO BASKET WEAVE

Weave the leather cord over and under the three wire rings. Be sure the cord stays tight. Repeat, weaving back and forth, until the ring is covered. Then tuck in any loose ends.

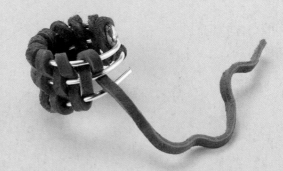

Capstone Young Readers are published by
Capstone, 1710 Roe Crest Drive,
North Mankato, Minnesota 56003.

www.capstoneyoungreaders.com

Library of Congress Cataloging-in-Publication Data
Cataloging-in-publication information is on file with the
Library of Congress.
ISBN 978-1-62370-645-6 (paperback)
ISBN 978-1-62370-646-3 (eBook PDF)

Editors: Mari Bolte and Alesha Halvorson
Designer: Tracy Davies McCabe
Project Creators: Marcy Morin, Sarah Schuette, and Lori Blackwell
Art Director: Heather Kindseth
Media Researcher: Morgan Walters
Premedia Specialist: Kathy McColley

Photo Credits:
All photos by Capstone Press:
Karon Dubke

Artistic Effects:
Shutterstock: ganpanjanee, design element, Ozerina Anna, design
element, Stephanie Zieber, design element, Vaclav Mach, design element

Printed and bound in China.
009610F16